COLO

Winter Wonderland

new seasons®
a division of Publications International, Ltd.

Louis Weber, CEO
Publications International, Ltd.
8140 Lehigh Ave
Morton Grove, IL 60053

Images from Shutterstock.com

Permission is never granted for commercial purposes.

ISBN: 978-1-63938-900-1

Manufactured in China.

8 7 6 5 4 3 2 1

Let's get social!

 @Publications_International

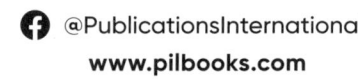 @PublicationsInternational
www.pilbooks.com

Bundle Up

Home is where the heat is

KEEP WARM
AND
DRINK
COCOA

COLD HANDS warm HEART

EXPLORE THE GREAT indoors

CHILLIN WITH MY SNOWMIES

Snow DAYS *Are The* BEST DAYS

Life is Better With Snow